THE ART OF
Upcycle

REPURPOSE, RECLAIM &
REDEFINE LEISURE TIME

2013

www.absolutebodo.com

THE ART OF
Upcycle

REPURPOSE, RECLAIM & REDEFINE LEISURE TIME

enjoy

MORE
INSPIRED
DIY PROJECTS

with Linda Bodo

ABSOLUTE BODO

Printed in Canada

Cataloguing data available from Library and Archives Canada

Published by Absolute Bodo
Edmonton, Alberta, Canada

Publication management: Bruce Timothy Keith
Editor: Lee Craig
Book and cover design: Carol Dragich, Dragich Design
Photography: Akemi Matsubuchi

DISCLAIMER
Because of differing conditions, materials, tools, and individual skills,
Linda Bodo and Absolute Bodo assume no responsibility for any
damages, injuries suffered or losses incurred as a result of attempting
any projects in this book. Always read and observe safety precautions
provided by manufacturers, and follow all accepted safety procedures.

DEDICATION

For H.

Contents

Introduction   *xiii*

   The Bold and the Boler   *xv*

   About the Projects   *xviii*

Quick Picks

A-Skew   2

Bottled Up   3

Bottled Up   5

CANapes   6

CANdle Power   7

Magnetic Personalities   8

Primpcess Mirror   9

Smarty Plants   10

Sold on Solder   11

Quick Picks

Spoonerism   12

Tote-ally Awesome   14

Tray Bien   16

UnCANny Clock   18

Water under the Ridge   19

Wine Spine   20

Window Dressing   22

Wobblers   23

Zip It Up   24

Main Projects

Adrift   26

Cateau   34

Chadder   40

Main Projects

Counter Intelligence 46

Flat*wear* 52

Head*STRONG* 58

Horsing Around 64

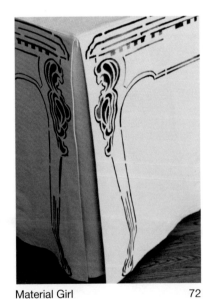

Material Girl 72

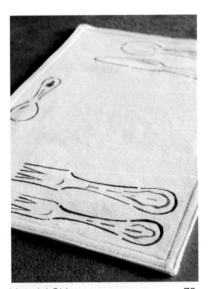

Material Girl 79

Monkey Business 80

Ruff Day 86

Some Like It Haute 94

Suitable Impression 100

Swiss Movements 106

Do It Yourself 113

   Safety Do's and Don'ts 115

   Doing It Right 116

   Timberrrrr 117

   The Tile File 118

   Sticky Situations 120

   Paints and Tints 120

Index 123

Acknowledgements 126

Introduction

Dad knew how to salvage materials and give them a second life. He even knew how to repurpose the second life and create something entirely new from its contents. Before going green was cool, he reduced, reused and recycled. Dad was ahead of his time, but his penchant for resurrecting relics was innate. The recycling process, after all, traces back thousands of years.

For me, recycling has always been a way of life. Raised by European parents, I know a thing or two about repurposing. Leftover bones were tossed in a pot to make soup stock, retired suits were stitched into quilts, orphaned buttons were collected in empty chocolate tins, and tissue was ironed and saved for the next gift—which, of course, was handmade. Toys, clothing and games were all made in-house, often with reclaimed items that had outlived their original purpose.

Travel has also played an important role in my life, offering me a glimpse into various people's lifestyles. I've always been impressed by how other cultures reinvest in their environment with creative ingenuity:

An obelisk fashioned from rusted garden tools complements an English country garden. A chandelier of mismatched cutlery adds whimsy to a Provençal kitchen. Chairs tailored from cable spools encourage relaxation on a Tuscan loggia. A damaged Herend platter enjoys new life as a mosaic table top in a Hungarian drawing room.

They do not let their waste "waste" away; instead they transform rubbish into something of greater value, be it functional or ornamental. Those experiences, along with my affinity for recycling, inspired me to kick recycle up a notch into the art of "upcycle." Partnered with the resurgence of the handmade movement in recent years, the fusion of repurposing and hand-crafting items has formed the backbone of this book.

Repurpose, reclaim and redefine leisure time. Saving money and our planet aren't the only objectives; self-fulfillment and stress relief are fundamental do-it-yourself values. If you have an hour or a weekend, *The Art of Upcycle* has a project guaranteed to take DIY to DI*Wise*. Start with baby steps and reduce your footprint on the earth by redirecting items destined for our landfills into limited edition, handmade projects guaranteed to turn heads. And don't forget to have fun along the way.

THE BOLD AND THE BOLER

Boldly, I stuck to my guns. Amidst all the flak from family and friends, I refused to falter. *What do they know?* I reasoned. *I have a vision.*

I fell in love with the little egg-shaped trailers during my family's RV travels. I vowed to acquire my very own Boler someday. My dream was to Bodo-fy the unit into a sexy leopard print ensemble that would accompany me to presentations and book signings. The more I thought about it, the more I wanted it. I was a woman possessed.

My husband, H., went down south a few days to golf with the guys, and I knew I had a small window of opportunity. The plan was to purchase the wheels before his return and realize my dream. The only way I would become the proud owner of a Boler would be if the darn thing was just parked in the driveway upon his return and maybe, just maybe, I had lost the receipt.

I sourced a 1974 beige-on-beige number and wasted no time contacting the owner in a sleepy little town an hour away. It was still available, and I raced out there immediately. As I drove up the mile-long driveway through acres of canola, I wondered what kind of shape the Boler would be in. It didn't matter—as soon as I rounded the corner and saw her nestled in the yard-high grass it was, well, love at first sight. Despite the stench of pee and 35 years of dust in the Boler, I plunked down my cash. A few days later my acquisition was delivered. I giggled uncontrollably while rummaging in forgotten drawers and creaky cabinets and began plotting the makeover. I could already see us bounding down the highway and taking the West by storm.

As I peeled back layers of materials, I envisioned the family vacations once spent in my little egg: warm summer days of sandcastles and triple-decker ice cream cones between dips in the lake, followed by evenings of toasted marshmallows and shooting stars before falling asleep to the hoo-hoo-hoot of the great horned owl. Sadly, the little trailer that was, was no longer. Years of neglect, hostile feral takeovers and the dawn of the super-sized RV seemed to have stripped away any dignity the Boler once enjoyed—never mind that she was fathered from a septic tank blueprint. Armed with rubber gloves and a respirator, I stripped away the upholstery, carpeting and curtains and scrubbed every crevice and orifice with high-octane cleansers. Slowly but surely the odour gradually dissipated; any lingering aromas were chased away with lavender essential oils.

Before performing any plastic surgery, I took my baby into the garage for a full check-up and spa treatment. She spent three weeks at the infirmary before she was considered roadworthy. Tires, repacked axel bearings, kitchen taps, regulators, a POW-R-SURGE battery, a fridge and a myriad of seals and gaskets brought her up to snuff—along with an invoice that surpassed the original bill of sale. Then came the process of decorating and skinning. A few minor technicalities intervened occasionally: cracked hoses, a rusted hitch, broken lenses and a warped door were beginning to take their toll on my patience and my pocketbook. Then there was the time I was working in the Boler in the garage and she moved, just ever so slightly. But it was enough to prevent the door from opening and I was trapped. It would be hours before H. was due home, and I had left my cellphone on the work bench. Gently, I began rocking the trailer back and forth until we had gathered enough momentum to roll out the garage door. I watched in horror as we picked up speed and sailed into the wrought-iron fence. Fortunately, damage was minimal.

Well, she's been prodded, poked and pelted for six months now, but the BodoBoler is finally *almost* finished.

BOLER FACTS

The Boler ultra-light fibreglass trailer was invented in Winnipeg in 1968 by Ray Olecko, a car salesman and inventor. An interest in fibreglass led him to patent a septic tank design with tapered ends. The invention was a hit thanks to its ease of transport when compared to its concrete and steel cousins. While camping with his family one summer, Ray came up with the idea of tweaking the tank concept into a lightweight camper that was easy to tow and move around. The prototype reminded him of a hat—more specifically, a bowler, and thus the Boler was born.

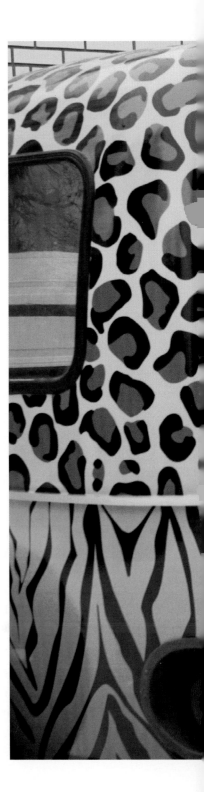

REPURPOSE, RECLAIM & REDEFINE LEISURE TIME

○ simple

◑ intermediate

● challenging

COST
$25–35
(SRP $200–275)

TIME
4–6 hours

MEASUREMENTS

Metric is the official standard of measurement in Canada, but lumber, pipe, hardware and tools are still sold in imperial measures. For this reason, all of my projects are created using imperial measurements.

SKILL LEVEL

I've rated each project according to difficulty (simple, intermediate and challenging). You can tell which is which by following the graphic legend to the left.

TIME AND COST

I've also provided a rough time investment for creating each project, estimated the DIY cost for materials and assigned a suggested retail price (SRP) value.

Quick Picks

A-Skew 2

Bottled Up 3

Bottled Up 5

CANapes 6

CANdle Power 7

Magnetic Personalities 8

Primpcess Mirror 9

Smarty Plants 10

Sold on Solder 11

Spoonerism 12

Tote-ally Awesome 14

Tray Bien 16

UnCANny Clock 18

Water under the Ridge 19

Wine Spine 20

Window Dressing 22

Wobblers 23

Zip It Up 24

A-Skew

COST
$10–15

TIME
1–2 hours

A recycled olive oil tin and bamboo skewers will house slicing supplies with style. This knife block saves you from having to aim at predetermined slots. Bundle the leftover ends of bamboo with raffia or string and use them as fire starters.

MATERIALS
Olive oil tins (one for each knife block)

Styrofoam packing, ½–1" thick, trimmed to fit bottom of tin

Bamboo skewers (about 12 packages of 12" skewers)

Electrical tape

Elastic bands

TOOLS
Can opener

Metal file

Handsaw or band saw

Tape measure

Goggles

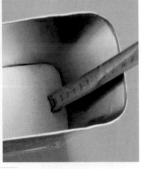

STEP BY STEP

1. Apply two layers of electrical tape around outside top of tin (to protect tin from marring by can opener). Remove tin lid and file down any sharp edges on inside of tin. Remove electrical tape. Clean inside of tin with detergent.

2. Line bottom of tin with Styrofoam and measure distance from Styrofoam to top of tin to determine skewer lengths.

3. Bundle each package of skewers with elastic bands (to ease cutting), and cut to length.

4. Lay tin on its side and pack in skewers (blunt ends towards bottom) as tightly as possible.

○ ● ○

Bottled Up

COST
$3–5

TIME
3 hours

Pair empty bottles with recycled bed springs or handmade coils to create this funky floral funnel, or use a wine crate to display a trio of bottles. The perfect gift for any oenophile.

MATERIALS
Bed springs or
11-gauge bottom wire
(chainlink fence wire,
available at hardware
outlets)

Wine bottles

Corks

9" x 15" x ½" plywood
or wine crates

20-gauge wire

1" x 1" x 4' wood slat

Hot glue sticks

Wine sleeves (available
at wine-making stores)

2" screws and plugs

TOOLS
7" wet tile saw

Rotary tool with file
attachment (optional)

150-grit and
220-grit sandpaper

Stapler, with ½" heavy duty
staples

Glue gun

Utility knife

Tape measure

Wire cutters

Drill, ¹⁄₁₆" drill bit and
1¼" spade bit

Pencil

Jigsaw

Needle-nose pliers

Goggles, gloves and
ear protection

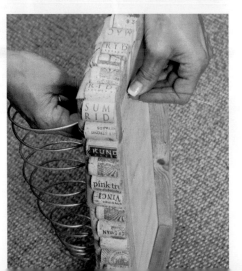

STEP BY STEP

CORKBOARD

1. Wash bottles, remove labels. Adjust tile saw to cut bottles $3/4$–1" from bottom. Turn on saw and slowly move bottle towards rotating blade. Roll bottle against blade in one continuous motion to score bottle. Do not cut through. Slowly draw bottle closer and closer to blade until the glass has been cut. Sand with 150-grit sandpaper and finish with 220-grit or with rotary tool fitted with file attachment.

2. Force cork as deeply as possible into bottle neck and cover with wine sleeve. Run hot water over sleeve to shrink into place to seal bottle neck. Set aside.

3. Cut two 15" and two $7\frac{1}{2}$" wood slats. Hot glue slats around edge of plywood. Cut corks in half lengthwise to save on number of corks, if needed. Hot glue corks onto face and sides of plywood.

4. If using 11-gauge wire, wrap a 10' length around a bottle to create a cradle and position wire in place on corkboard. If using a bed spring, adjust coils with needle-nose pliers to fit bottle profile.

5. Drill $1/16$" holes through corkboard and insert loops of 20-gauge wire to secure coils.

6. Attach a length of 20-gauge wire to back of corkboard with staples. Hang on wall and lower bottle into cradle.

STEP BY STEP

WINE CRATE

1. Prepare wine bottles as in first and second steps of corkboard instructions.

2. Remove crate lid. Position bottles on one long side of crate in desired locations. Mark bottle locations and mark openings for bottle necks on other long side of crate.

3. Drill $1^{1}/_{4}$" holes with spade bit for bottle necks. Drill pilot holes in other side of crate with spade bit and enlarge openings to desired sizes with jigsaw to accommodate bottle bodies.

4. Sand or file any rough edges.

5. Attach crate to a wall with screws and plugs so that large holes are on top. Insert bottles upside down through crate. Fill interior of crate with shredded packing material.

CANapes

● ○ ○

COST
$1

TIME
15 minutes

These squirrel-proof feeders are the ultimate recycling project for discarded tuna tins and meat renderings. They are perfect for attracting smaller birds into your yard during winter.

MATERIALS
Selection of small, wide tins (e.g., tuna)

Coat hanger

Chopstick

Beef, pork or chicken rendering

Bird seed or dried fruit and nuts

Metal ornament, holes drilled top and bottom for suspension (optional)

Electrical tape

TOOLS
Awl

Wire cutters

Pliers

STEP BY STEP

1. Cut coat hanger into 6" lengths. Fashion a hook at one end of each length.

2. Puncture side of tin with awl and insert hanger. Bend inside end of hanger to secure. Cover hole with electrical tape to prevent heated rendering from leaking until it has set. If using a metal ornament detail on hanger, cut wire into two 3" lengths and wire ornament onto tin.

3. Melt rendering and mix with sunflower seeds, dried fruit and/or nuts in a one-to-one ratio. Pour into prepared tins on a plate lined with paper towel. Freeze until set.

4. Keep frozen until ready to use. Hang outside when birds need a snack on a chilly day. Cut chopstick to length and insert into feeder for a perch.

CANdle Power

COST
$5–10

TIME
3–4 hours

MATERIALS
Large can
Hanging lamp kit
Variety of spoons
Printed labels
Floral wire or
24-gauge wire

TOOLS
Drill, ¹/₁₆" and
¹/₂" drill bits
Wire cutters
Double-sided tape
Scissors
Tape measure
Marker
Goggles

Mismatched spoons *can* create a *souper* pendant. This inexpensive light is perfect for small spaces and tight budgets—the ideal solution for college dorms or a first apartment.

STEP BY STEP

1. Scan or computer-generate a soup label sized to cover can. Print in two sections, if necessary, and adhere together with double-sided tape. Laminate for durability, if desired, and trim to size.

2. Drill ¹/₂" hole at centre top of can and several ¹/₁₆" holes around centre for ventilation.

3. Drill ¹/₁₆" holes around bottom circumference of can and through handle of each spoon.

4. Install lamp kit according to package instructions.

5. Adhere label to can with double-sided tape.

6. Wire spoons to bottom of can.

Magnetic Personalities

COST
$35–95

TIME
2–3 hours

Transform your fridge from the ordinary to the extraordinary with a giant magnet.

MATERIALS
Magnetic sheeting (available through sign supply outlets)

Image saved to disc at 300 pixels per inch

TOOLS
Utility knife

Spray bottle filled with soapy water (1 part dish detergent, 5 parts water)

Wallpaper squeegee or credit card wrapped with paper towel

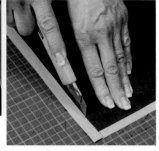

STEP BY STEP

1. Cut magnetic sheeting with utility knife to fit fridge.

2. Send image file to sign supplier and order print on self-adhesive vinyl slightly larger than magnetic sheet.

3. Peel off 6" of vinyl image from one side and remove backing with scissors. Mist exposed adhesive side of image generously with soapy water.

4. Position image on magnetic sheet with slight overlap on top and sides. Slowly squeegee vinyl down with wallpaper tool or credit card to remove all air and liquid from under vinyl.

5. Continue to remove backing 6" at a time, misting with soapy water and then squeezing air bubbles and moisture from backing.

6. Trim excess vinyl around edges and apply magnet to fridge.

Primpcess Mirror

○○○

COST
$15–25

TIME
2–3 hours

See yourself crowned with a tiara while primping with this mirror designed for a princess. Recycle an old mirror to keep costs down and use etched, self-adhesive vinyl instead of toxic creams or sandblasting.

MATERIALS
Mirror

Etched self-adhesive vinyl (available at sign supply outlets, sold by the foot)

Costume jewels and gemstones (purchase pre-glued variety to avoid using super glue)

Gel super glue (if not using the pre-glued gemstones)

Scrap paper

TOOLS
Scissors

Pencil

Tape measure

Needle-nose pliers

STEP BY STEP

1. Sketch a tiara on scrap paper and cut out. For a symmetrical crown, fold paper in half before cutting design.

2. Trace design onto etched vinyl. Cut out tiara.

3. Remove backing from etched vinyl and apply to centre of top third of mirror. Use a stiff plastic card to press vinyl firmly onto mirror, dispelling any air bubbles.

4. Affix costume jewels or gemstones as desired with needle-nose pliers. If gemstones are not pre-glued kind, apply gel glue sparingly to prevent seepage.

Smarty Plants

COST
$2–3

TIME
1 hour

Professionals use floral tape to make a grid at the vase opening to hold stems upright when they arrange fresh flowers. This process is time-consuming, and the tape is generally tossed out after one application. Create your own reusable grid by repurposing stucco mesh into a cover that can be kicked up a notch with a little bling.

MATERIALS
Square vases
1/2" stucco mesh
Beads, baubles and tassels
24-gauge wire

TOOLS
Wire cutters
Gloves
Goggles
Needle-nose pliers

STEP BY STEP

1. Cut mesh 1/2" larger than top of vase on all sides. Cut off corners at 45-degree angle.

2. Centre mesh over vase and fold down edges for snug fit.

3. Decorate mesh with beads, baubles or tassels. Fill bottom of vase with glass stones or marbles for added stem stability.

Sold on Solder

COST
$5–10

TIME
1–3 hours

MATERIALS
Lead-free solder
(50/50) or heavy-
gauge wire

Flux

Copper pennies

Small bowls or
dishes

Tea lights and tea
light holders

TOOLS
Solder gun

Wire cutters

Needle-nose
pliers

Tape measure

Goggles

Small brush
(for applying flux)

Fashion solder or heavy-gauge wire into functional accessories with a twist.

STEP BY STEP

SOAP SAVER

1. Coil a length of solder or wire
   to fit in bottom of soap dish as
   soap-drying rack.

STEP BY STEP

TEA LIGHT CRADLES

1. Cut two 20" lengths of solder.

2. Coat one side of a penny with
   flux. Centre one solder length
   on penny and solder in place.
   Centre second solder length on
   penny perpendicular to first and
   solder in place.

3. Centre tea light on bare side of
   penny and bend solder pieces
   upwards to hug tea light. Coil
   ends of solder and fit into tea
   light holder.

Spoonerism

○○○

COST
$10–20

TIME
1–2 hours

Fill this squirrel-proof feeder with black oil sunflower seeds to encourage smaller birds into your yard. The extended roof will shelter diners from rain or shine. Put the feeder in a tree where branches offer birds a safe haven from predators.

MATERIALS
2, 8" x 12" block ends, 28 gauge (look in ventilation department of hardware stores)

2, 8" x 10" block ends, 28 gauge

$1/2$" x $1 1/2$" hexagonal nuts and bolts, 4 sets

4 x $1/2$" copper couplings (look in plumbing department of hardware stores)

8 large washers

20-gauge wire

Wire coat hanger

Ladle

Scrap plywood (approximately 4" x 4")

TOOLS
Drill, $1/2$" metal bit

Pencil

Felt pen

Tape measure

Straight edge

Scrap wood

Clamp

Wire cutters

Gloves

Goggles

Needle-nose pliers

STEP BY STEP

1. Mark positions for four holes (for bolts) on lower portion of 8" x 12" block ends.

2. Create a 4" x 4" jig (template) from scrap plywood and transfer marked positions from block end to jig. Drill $1/2$" hole on each mark.

3. Place one large block end on scrap wood and centre jig with holes over marked positions on block end. Clamp together to prevent drill bit from chattering across metal. Drill all four holes. Drill hole for ladle. Repeat with second 8" x 12" block end.

4. Attach block ends front to back by slipping a bolt, washer, coupling, washer and nut through walls. Repeat with each hole.

5. Fold down top edges of block ends and slip 20-gauge wire under lips for suspension. Attach 8" x 10" block ends as roof units and pinch grooves to secure in place.

6. Cut ladle to length, if desired, and insert into feeder.

7. Cut neck off wire hanger and straighten. Curl ends with needle-nose pliers and fold in centre. Slip under suspension wire.

8. Hang feeder in yard and fill ladle with black oil sunflower seeds to attract small birds.

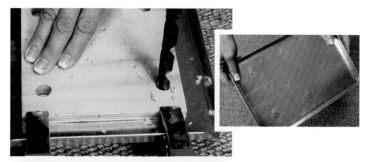

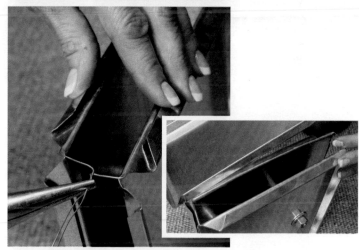

Tote-ally Awesome

COST
$5–10

TIME
3–4 hours

Be fashionably green and avoid charges for plastic bags on your next shopping excursion by using this custom tote. Created from salvaged bubble wrap and an old pair of jeans, this project "upcycles" materials to the max.

MATERIALS

Bubble wrap

Embroidery floss

Sewing thread

Old jeans

Rivets or screw posts (available at leather craft or craft stores)

4 x 1" solid D-rings (available at leather craft or craft stores)

5" x 15" heavy cardboard, with edges rounded off

TOOLS

Scissors

Embroidery needle

Tape measure

Sewing machine

Awl

Small clips or clothespins

STEP BY STEP

1. Cut six pieces of bubble wrap: two 16" x 45" (for main compartment) and four 6" x 20" (for side panels).

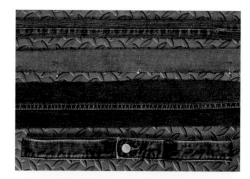

2. Remove waistband from jeans and adjust to fit around top edge of tote (approximately 42").

3. Cut four pieces of denim: two 3" x 48" lengths for straps, and two 3" x 30" lengths for handles. (Sew together smaller pieces to make these lengths, if necessary). For each strap and handle, fold pieces right sides together and stitch along length. Turn inside out, press and topstitch if desired.

4. Hand or machine-stitch a D-ring onto each end of both straps.

5. Line up two main compartment pieces of bubble wrap on top of each other, textured surfaces together. Do the same with each set of side panels. Form a sac by attaching front and back together with sides pieces. Hold bubble wrap together with clips or clothespins and then use blanket stitch and embroidery floss to sew pieces together.

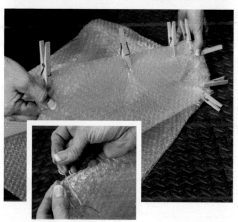

6. Hand or machine-stitch waistband around top of tote to strengthen opening and to provide strong attachments for straps.

7. Insert cardboard bottom.

8. Position straps around outside of tote, 4" in from sides. Attach straps to bottom of tote with rivets or posts through cardboard. Attach ends of straps to waistband with rivets or posts.

9. Hand or machine-stitch handles onto strap D-rings.

Tray Bien

COST
$5–10
(for a set of four)

TIME
2–3 hours

Scrumptious appetizers sail by as you juggle a wine glass in one hand and a plate in the other. Alleviate the problem of eating while drinking with this convenient tray. If you want to add a bit of colour, dye the tray with food colouring and seal it with beeswax.

MATERIALS
Small cutting boards (available at discount dollar stores)

Beeswax or salad bowl finish

Exterior wood glue

Hot glue sticks

Corks

Scrap two-by-four (for jig)

Bamboo skewers or 11-gauge bottom wire (chainlink fence wire), for optional skewers

TOOLS
Jigsaw

Drill or drill press, 1½" Forstner bit

Glue gun

Band saw

Sander, 180-grit sandpaper

Utility knife

Tack cloth

Pencil

Gloves

Goggles

Needle-nose pliers

Wire cutters

STEP BY STEP

TRAY

1. Mark $1^1/_2$" in from edge at centre of long side of board.

2. Drill through board with Forstner bit. Mark from outside edge to bored hole a channel wide enough to accommodate a wine glass stem. Cut channel with jigsaw. Sand. Wipe with tack cloth.

3. Create a jig to cut corks in half by channelling $1/_2$" wide and $1/_2$" deep groove down centre of a scrap piece of two-by-four. Clamp jig to band saw directly in front of blade. Place cork on jig channel and carefully push against blade to begin cutting. Feed cork through blade by pushing back end of cork with next cork so fingers do not get near rotating blade. Continue process until all corks are halved.

4. Glue corks around edge of board using both wood glue and hot glue. Hot glue will hold corks in place until wood glue has set. Angle-cut corks that border stem channel to allow glasses to pass through more easily. Dry overnight and seal with several coats of beeswax.

5. Add detail to handle by attaching a champagne cork, if desired.

6. Hand wash and re-seal periodically.

APPETIZER SKEWERS
1. Cut bamboo skewers to 4–6" long and insert into corks.

or

1. Cut 11-gauge wire to 8–10" long. Coil one end with needle-nose pliers. Snug up cork next to coiled end and gently curve wire with pliers. Slightly sharpen tip with sandpaper.

UnCANny Clock

● ○ ○

COST
$10–15

TIME
2–3 hours

This whimsical whisked piece is timely for any kitchen. Ask a local restaurant to save you a large tin if you don't normally purchase such large quantities of canned goods.

MATERIALS
Large tin
Pendulum clock movement (available at hobby or craft stores)
Small, lightweight wire whisk
Novelty clock hands (available at craft stores, optional)
Wood paint stir stick
Double-sided tape

TOOLS
Drill, $^{11}/_{32}$" drill bit
Wire cutters
Handsaw
Tape measure
Marker
Scissors
Goggles

STEP BY STEP

1. Drill $^{11}/_{32}$" hole in centre front of can for clock movement.

2. Cut stir stick to fit between top and bottom lips of can. Fix to back of can with double-sided tape. (Stir stick will prevent clock from wobbling when pendulum is swinging.)

3. Drill $^{11}/_{32}$" hole through wood and can, approximately 1" down from top (for suspension).

4. Place two strips of double-sided tape on front of clock movement. Attach movement according to package instructions and replace hands with novelty set, if desired.

5. Pull out looped end of whisk from coiled neck to create a hook and attach to pendulum latch.

Water under the Ridge

COST
$1–2

TIME
1 hour

MATERIALS
Empty bottles with caps
Small porcelain vases
4" x 4" or 2" x 2" tiles

TOOLS
Rotary tool, diamond-tipped bit and fine grinder
Gloves
Goggles
Mask
Tape measure
Felt pen
Porcelain and china weld adhesive

Take bottle recycling to a new level: repurpose water or juice bottles into playful stacked vessels. Create a series of these vases to display single blooms in profusion.

STEP BY STEP

1. Turn vase upside down and drill hole in bottom with diamond drill bit. (Start rotary tool on slow speed and gradually increase speed until you have penetrated through porcelain.) Enlarge opening slightly to accommodate grinder bit and expand opening until it is the same aperture as the bottle mouth. Wipe clean.

2. Measure centre of tile and mark with felt pen. Repeat drilling and grinding process with tile, starting on unglazed side. Drill coordinating hole in bottle cap.

3. Adhere tile, vase and cap together with porcelain glue and cure 24 hours before using.

Wine Spine

●○○

COST
$4–5

TIME
1–2 hours

Glide easily through your mingling guests without spilling a drop. Slits and slots keep the glasses and bottle upright.

MATERIALS
1" x 6" x 4' pine board
Craft paint (optional)
Wax or Varathane
Corks
2" wood screws
Glue sticks

TOOLS
Jigsaw
Drill, small drill bit
Glue gun
Paint brush (optional)
Pencil
Tape measure
Sander, 180-grit sandpaper
Cloth
Straight edge
Gloves
Goggles

STEP BY STEP

1. Cut board in half to get two 24" long pieces.

2. Lay out four glasses and wine bottle along centre of one board. Mark off circular opening for bottle 3" from one end and a slot for glass stems at other end. Ensure openings are large enough to accommodate various sizes of bottles and glasses.

3. Cut slot for glass stems with jigsaw. Drill pilot hole for bottle opening; cut out with jigsaw.

4. Sand wood and wipe. Paint if desired. To achieve a pickled finish, water down paint by 50 per cent, brush on paint and wipe off with a damp cloth.

5. Glue corks around edge of bottom board, leaving one end open for glass stem slot and a 2" gap centred at other end.

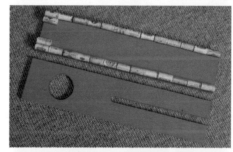

6. Glue top board onto corks. Flip unit over and pre-drill 10 pilot holes for screws (to prevent wood from splitting). Screw top to bottom with 2" screws.

7. Varathane or wax finished unit.

Window Dressing

COST
$5–10

TIME
2–3 hours

Dress up any window with café-style curtains detailed with small test tube pockets—the perfect digs for single blooms. These sheer window dressings are guaranteed to make you smile with every glance outside. You can whip up this project for next to nothing by recycling an existing curtain and saved floral tubes, vanilla bean tubes or cigar tubes.

MATERIALS
Sheer stiff fabric (organza or drapery fabric), enough to cover window plus hems and another 12" for pockets

Thread

Test tubes

Curtain rod

Brackets

TOOLS
Scissors

Sewing machine

Tape measure

Pins

Iron

Cloth or towel

STEP BY STEP

1. Cut fabric to size 1" wider and 3" longer than window. Roll $1/4$" hem on sides and bottom and sew 1" sleeve at top for rod. Steam press, using a damp cloth on fabric to prevent scorching.

2. Cut several $2^1/2$" wide strips of fabric (with grain), and hem $1/4$" on long sides. Press. Cut sewn strips into $4^1/2$" units and hem top and bottom.

3. Lay out pockets on curtain, pin in place and sew. Insert test tubes.

4. Feed rod through sleeve and hang in place. Fill tubes with water and add blooms.

Wobblers

COST
$2–3

TIME
1–2 hours

Wobblers are vessels that weeble, but never fall over. These little delights combine round wooden coasters or slices of tree trunks with tubes to accommodate flowers. Place these wobblers outside where a gentle breeze will keep them rocking and rolling.

MATERIALS
Large test tubes, vanilla bean tubes or cigar tubes (approximately 6" long)

Round wooden coasters, tree trunk discs ($^3/_4$" x $4^1/_2$") or scrap wood ($^1/_4$–$^3/_4$" thick and large enough to make $4^1/_2$" diameter circles)

Craft paint (optional)

Wax or Varathane

Weather stripping

TOOLS
Jigsaw

Drill or drill press, spade bits of various sizes

Paint brush (optional)

Pencil

Tape measure

Sander, 180-grit sandpaper

Gloves

Goggles

STEP BY STEP

1. If using scrap wood pieces to make coasters, use jigsaw to cut $4^1/_2$" diameter discs.

2. Mark centre of coaster or disc and bore a hole with appropriate spade bit slightly larger than diameter of test tube. Sand and wipe clean. Line inside of bored hole with weather stripping to ensure a snug fit for the tube.

3. Finish with two coats of paint, if desired, and seal with two coats of Varathane or wax to prevent wood from swelling if it becomes wet.

4. Add test tubes, fill with water and add your favourite blooms.

Zip It Up

●○○

COST
$2–5

TIME
1–2 hours

Dress up a vase with a false zippered covering. Use a recycled zipper pull and brass tabs for the teeth.

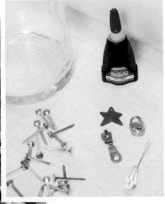

MATERIALS
Etched vinyl (available at sign supply outlets)

Zipper pull and ornamental charm

1" brass fasteners

Round vase

Gel super glue

Scrap paper (for template)

TOOLS
Scissors

Wire cutters

Pencil

Tape measure

Spray bottle filled with soapy water

Credit card

Utility knife

Needle-nose pliers

STEP BY STEP

1. Cut vinyl ¹/₄" wider than circumference of vase and ¹/₂" shorter than height of vase. Remove backing to expose adhesive side and spray generously with soapy water.

2. Apply vinyl to vase ¹/₄" down from top edge.

3. Using a hard, flat item, such as a credit card, press out air bubbles from vinyl. Wipe excess moisture away with a paper towel.

4. Cut a V-shape from scrap paper at desired size for zippered opening. Trace outline of V-shape onto vinyl with pencil. Cut away V-shape from vinyl with utility knife.

5. Using wire cutters, cut brass fasteners in half to create false zipper teeth. Put a small amount of gel glue on zipper teeth and fix to vase using needle-nose pliers.

6. Glue on zipper pull and attach charm.

Main Projects

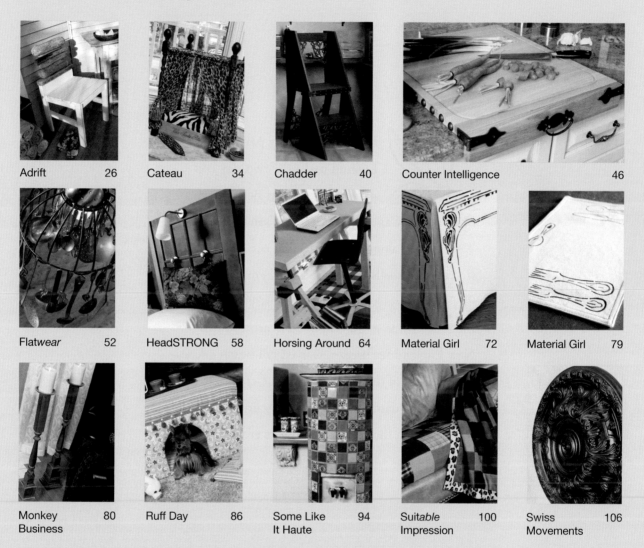

Adrift 26

Cateau 34

Chadder 40

Counter Intelligence 46

Flatwear 52

HeadSTRONG 58

Horsing Around 64

Material Girl 72

Material Girl 79

Monkey Business 80

Ruff Day 86

Some Like It Haute 94

Suitable Impression 100

Swiss Movements 106

Adrift

Every summer my parents and I would make the two-day trip in our Volkswagen Beetle from Montreal to Cape Cod's stretch of sandy beaches. We motored alongside spectacular ocean shores strewn with shells and the skeletal remains of sea life. Massive rocks slick with algae stretched into the water while seagulls bobbed nearby. Warm New England sea breezes swayed tall beach grasses in hundreds of tidal flats where blue crabs left their mark on the damp, firm sand—a grainy carpet textured with the undulating prints etched by a receding tide.

These unique chairs are perfect for the patio, for picnics or for vacations by the sea.

DI_Wise_
Construct these organic chairs with flea market finds and stockpiled driftwood.

DIY
$25–35 (SRP $200–275)

○ ○ ●

COST
$25–35
(SRP $200–275)

TIME
4–6 hours

MATERIALS

Wooden, armless chair

Driftwood pieces (2–3" diameter x 12–18" long)

$1/2$" steel threaded rod, 36" long

8 x $1/2$" nuts

Paint, stain, oil, Varathane or wax (optional)

Two-by-four, 3' length

$2^1/2$" wood screws

Wood glue

Electrical tape

Mighty Putty

TOOLS

Drill or drill press, $1/16$" drill bit and $5/8$" and 1" spade bits

Sander, 150- and 220-grit sandpaper

Paint brush or roller and tray (if painting or staining wood)

Jigsaw or handsaw

Hacksaw

Clamps

Vise

Goggles

Gloves

File or rasp

STEP BY STEP

1. Stand two-by-four on its side and place against backrest supports. Mark height of two-by-four on backrest supports. Remove two-by-four and cut off chair back at marks.

2. Measure distance between backrest support stubs. Cut two-by-four to fit.

3. Measure 4" in from either end of cut two-by-four and mark at centre width of narrow side. Drill through two-by-four at marks using $^5/_8$" bit. Stand two-by-four on seat between backrest support stubs and clamp in place.

4. Using holes in two-by-four as guide, drill $^5/_8$" holes through seat. Unclamp and remove two-by-four.

5. Cut remaining piece of two-by-four to fit between seat supports on underside of seat directly under drilled holes. Glue two-by-four in place. Pre-drill pilot screw holes into two-by-four through chair sides using $^1/_{16}$" bit. Anchor two-by-four with $2^1/_2$" screws. Using holes in seat as a guide, drill $^5/_8$" holes through two-by-four under seat.

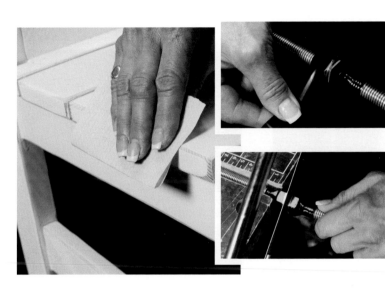

6. Glue and screw first two-by-four in place between backrest supports. Sand chair with 150-grit and then 220-grit sandpaper for a smooth finish. Finish chair as desired. To create an aged patina, hand sand all surfaces with 220-grit sandpaper, sanding additionally on edges and corners where typical wear and tear occurs. Clean, apply wax and buff.

7. Place two nuts at midpoint of threaded rod with just enough space between them to fit a hacksaw blade. Secure nuts in place with electrical tape. Place rod in vise and, with nuts acting as a guide for a straight cut, cut rod in half (for two 18" pieces). File any metal burrs and remove nuts on cut ends to re-channel threads.

8. Insert rods vertically through drilled holes in two-by-fours and seat. Add nuts under seat. (Rods will be held in place after you add first driftwood log.) Protect top rod ends with electrical tape to prevent marring threads as you add driftwood pieces.

9. Place a piece of driftwood across back of chair seat and mark location of rods. Drill ⁵/₈" holes through centre of driftwood at marks and gently slide onto rods. Repeat with remaining driftwood until 1¹/₂" of rod is left exposed at top. You may have to tailor some driftwood with sanding to ensure a tight fit to conceal rods.

10. *Optional:* Number driftwood logs so you can replace them after applying wax. Remove logs and finish with two coats of wax. Replace all pieces on rods except topper.

11. To create topper, drill half to three-quarters through one more driftwood log with 1" bit to accommodate nuts you will add to top of rods. Dry-fit topper and modify as needed.

12. Remove electrical tape and screw nuts onto rods to snug up driftwood.

13. Mix Mighty Putty following manufacturer's instructions. Fill bottom of bored holes on topper with putty. To prevent putty from oozing, do not overfill. Apply topper to top of chair. Clamp overnight.

Cateau

"Not *another* palace," Dad groaned. He had had his fill of traipsing through ostentatious castles. I, on the other hand, could not wait to penetrate the greatest piece of baroque architecture in Hungary: the Esterházy Palace in Fertöd. Entering the grounds through elaborate wrought-iron gates, we ascended a winding staircase punctuated by columns and statues. With tickets in hand, we donned the soft slip-ons over our shoes to avoid scuffing the polished marble floors, and we proceeded through the 121-plus rooms of the palace. On the upper levels, lavish rococo bedroom chambers featured magnificent porcelain stoves, designed to be stoked from hidden passages by servants to avoid disrupting any "blueblood beauty sleep." The beds themselves were ornately carved masterpieces, usually canopied with heavy, fringed brocade drapery. Braided silk pulls with generous tassels hung over gilt nightstands.

This canopied daybed may seem a bit over the top, but our pets deserve the best, after all.

DI*Wise*
Using spindles and a wine crate for this four poster bed adds a touch of class for your small four-legged friend.

DIY
$25–40 (SRP $125–150)
* For pets up to 10 lb.

COST
$25–40
(SRP $125–150)

TIME
4–5 hours

MATERIALS
4 spindles,
approximately 26" high
(available at Habitat for
Humanity Re-Stores,
architectural clearing
outlets)

4 small ball fence caps

Wine crate,
approximately
13" x 21" (available at
wine boutiques, liquor
stores, restaurants,
lounges and wine bars)

1½" wood screws

⅝" dowel, 6' length

1M upholstery fabric

1M sheer fabric

Thread

2 drapery tie backs

12" Velcro

Pillow (child or
travel size)

Stain/oil/wax; water-
based, non-toxic
(optional)

TOOLS
Sewing machine

Tape measure

Scissors

Drill, ¹/₁₆" and
⅝" drill bits

Wood glue

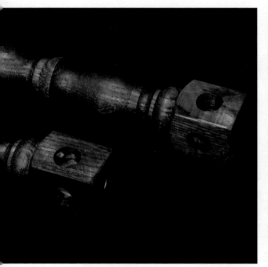   

STEP BY STEP

1. Drill $^5/_8$" holes $^1/_2$" deep on two adjacent sides of top of each spindle. Pre-drill pilot holes for fence balls on tops of spindles with $^1/_{16}$" bit.

2. Attach spindle bases to outside of crate with wood glue. Screw in place from inside corners of wine crate. Make sure bored holes at spindle tops face inwards.

3. Screw balls on spindles.

4. Cut four lengths of dowel measured 1" longer than distance between each pair of spindles.

5. Cut pillow front cover from washable fabric $^1/_2$" larger (on all sides) than pillow. Cut back with same measurements as front but add 8" to length. Cut back panel in half width-wise and fold edges over 2" on either side of centre cut. Press flat. With right sides facing up, overlap split back panels to match size of front. Pin back panels to front (right sides together), and stitch $^1/_2$" from edges all around perimeter. Turn right sides out. Add Velcro to the back overlap sections.

6. Cut sheer fabric for canopy according to illustrations. Hem all sides.

7. To make ³/₄" sleeves, fold fabric at **A** measurement plus ³/₄". Pin in place and stitch straight line ³/₄" in from edge of fold.

8. Stain, oil or wax crate and spindles as desired.

9. Place pillow in crate. Slide dowels through drape sleeves and insert into spindle tops. Secure drapes with tie backs on one side of bed to create opening.

³/₄" sleeve

| A | B | A | 2 x C *(Double measurement for gathering)* |

Cut 1

³/₄" sleeve

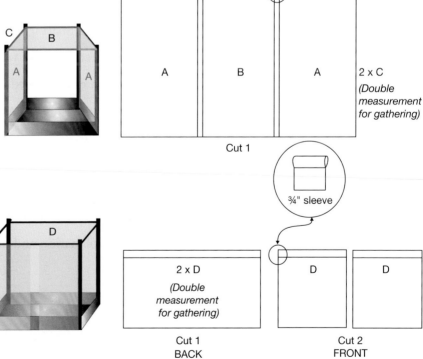

| 2 x D *(Double measurement for gathering)* | D | D |

Cut 1
BACK

Cut 2
FRONT

Chadder

A fine film of sand dusted our vehicle and glistened in shafts of sun that pierced the early morning haze. The Colorado Desert had been swallowed by the lush terrain of the Coachella Valley as Route 111 serpentined through towering palm grooves. Row upon row of date palms presided over the dale in an explosion of frond fireworks launched from pencil-thin trunks. Soaring up to 50 feet, these majestic trees need 10 to 15 years to reach maximum production of the prized Medjool dates. We spotted several boom lifts elevating palmeros into the tree tops, where they mounted rudimentary ladders permanently attached to the palms' crowns. Held in by a leather strap, these agile sky-walkers ascended into the frond core to perform a balancing act of propagation, pollination and harvesting.

This library chair serves double duty: a flip of the backrest transforms the chair into a ladder.

DI*Wise*
Use lumber from reclaimed furniture (tables, cabinets, chests) to keep costs manageable.

DIY
$25–50 (SRP $200–250)

COST
$25–50
(SRP $200–250)

TIME
4–6 hours

MATERIALS
Repurposed wooden unit (e.g., table, cabinet, chest)

Wood glue

14" piano hinge with screws

$1\frac{1}{2}$" finishing nails

Paint, stain or furniture wax (optional)

8, 8" x 7" wood or lightweight metal brackets with screws

Wood filler (optional)

Edging veneer, (optional)

TOOLS
Jigsaw

Sander, 180-grit sandpaper

Hammer

Drill, screw bit

Paint brush or cloth (depending method of finishing)

Tape measure

Pencil

Goggles

Gloves

REPURPOSE, RECLAIM & REDEFINE LEISURE TIME   43

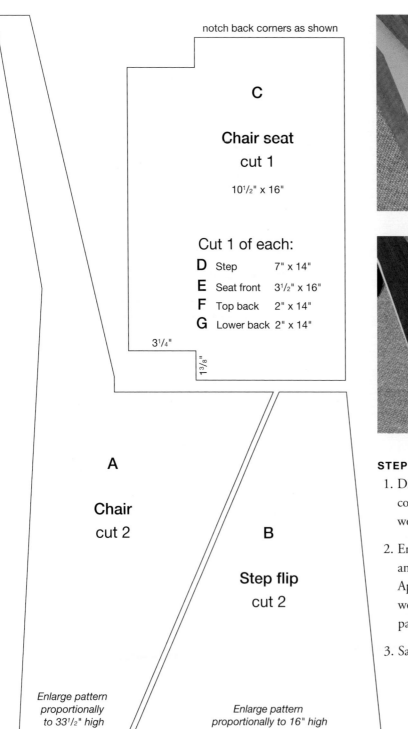

notch back corners as shown

C

Chair seat

cut 1

10¹/₂" x 16"

Cut 1 of each:

D Step   7" x 14"
E Seat front   3¹/₂" x 16"
F Top back   2" x 14"
G Lower back 2" x 14"

3¹/₄"

1³/₈"

A

Chair

cut 2

B

Step flip

cut 2

*Enlarge pattern
proportionally
to 33¹/₂" high*

*Enlarge pattern
proportionally to 16" high*

(approximately 445 per cent)

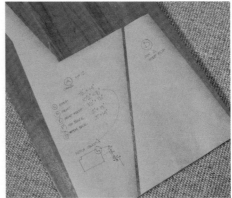

STEP BY STEP

1. Dismantle unit into individual components. Salvage any existing wood edging.

2. Enlarge illustrated outlines to size and use them to cut wood pieces. Apply edging veneer to raw edges of wood, if desired, according to veneer package instructions.

3. Sand pieces. Paint or finish as desired.

4. Screw brackets into designated areas. Using wood glue and finishing nails, assemble pieces as indicated in drawing.

5. Join seat sections with piano hinge.

6. Wax completed unit, if desired.

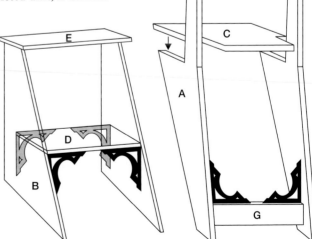

Counter Intelligence

The front desk clerk gave us directions to a well-known rendezvous he guaranteed would titillate our taste buds with traditional Haute Provence cuisine. My seat offered me a view into the heartbeat of the restaurant, where the lone chef single-handedly prepared meals for dozens of hungry patrons. An antique range simmered and sautéed delicious fare under the canopy of an aged copper hood. Tarnished pots and pans dangled from rough hewn beams, and an old stone sink held an army of dishes. A seasoned cutting board demonstrated years of wear, scarred by countless slices and dices. The auspicious absence of modern-day technology proved that fresh ingredients, simple cooking and family cordiality beat a Michelin rating any day.

This cutting board sports a lip that hugs your countertop, allowing it to glide across the surface with ease. Kick it up a notch with a collapsible sieve insert.

DI_Wise_
Use an existing wood cutting board and add hinges and a coordinating drawer pull.

DIY
$25–35 (SRP $125–200)

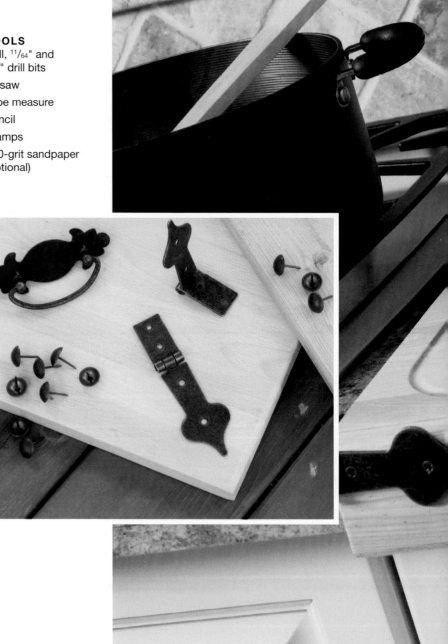

● ○ ○

COST
$25–35
(SRP $125–200)

TIME
1–2 hours

MATERIALS
Large breadboard
2 hinges
Drawer pull
1" x 3" pine board
(for lip), 2' length
Wood glue
Collapsible sieve
(optional)
Beeswax or olive oil
Upholstery studs
(optional)

TOOLS
Drill, $^{11}/_{64}$" and
$^{1}/_{16}$" drill bits
Jigsaw
Tape measure
Pencil
Clamps
220-grit sandpaper
(optional)

STEP BY STEP

1. Cut pine board to fit front (short side) of bread board. Dry-fit on countertop to make sure pine lip will not obstruct cabinet drawers. Attach drawer pull to centre of lip, pre-drilling $^{11}/_{64}$" holes for screws.

2. Glue lip to breadboard and clamp overnight.

3. Attach hinges to front corners as decoration, pre-drilling $^1/_{16}$" holes for screws. Embellish with upholstery studs if desired.

4. Finish breadboard and lip with two coats of wax or oil.

5. To incorporate collapsible sieve, measure internal diameter of sieve and mark appropriately sized circle in cutting board. Drill a pilot hole through board and then cut opening with jigsaw. Sand edges and insert sieve.

Flatwear

The four of us crammed into the pocket-sized rental car for an arduous journey through the Alpes-de-Provence. Our mission was to partake in the Sunday market in Digne-les-Bains some 90 kilometres away. Unfortunately, the breathtaking countryside demanded frequent stops. Several hours later we pried ourselves from the car, anxious to rummage through vendor wares on the main boulevard. Purveyors from nearby farms had us drooling over marinated olives, vine-wrapped goat cheese and golden lavender honey. We pined over tarnished doorknockers from an 18th-century chateau, lavishly monogrammed linens and stunning floral bouquets bound with hanks of raffia. Even though we were surrounded by a plenteous array of merchandise, we all left empty-handed—cramming one more item into the vehicle was out of the question.

Create an interesting kitchen chandelier with an assortment of ladles, spoons and sieves.

DI*Wise*
Flea markets and bazaars often carry antique kitchen paraphernalia; make sure your trunk is empty *before* heading out to market.

DIY
$25–75 (SRP $150–200)

●○○

COST
$25–75
(SRP $150–200)

TIME
4–6 hours

MATERIALS
Wire hanging flower basket

Hanging lamp kit, with bulb

Collection of spoons, forks and ladles

Metallic wax rub, pewter finish (optional; available at craft outlets)

26-gauge floral wire

Small metal mixing bowl or colander, approximately 6" diameter

TOOLS
Drill, $^3/_8$" and $^5/_{32}$" drill bits

Pliers

Gloves

Goggles

Wire cutters

Needle-nose pliers

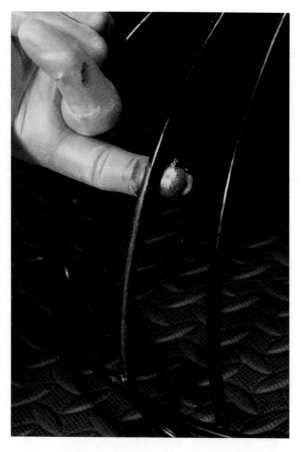

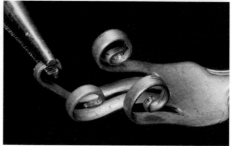

STEP BY STEP

1. Remove existing chain from basket. If desired, wax basket with pewter finish according to product directions.

2. Drill $5/32$" hole through end of each flatware handle. If using forks, curl tines with needle-nose pliers to avoid risk of injury from low-hanging fixtures.

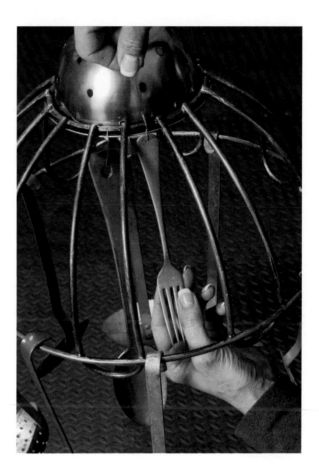

3. Drill ³/₈" hole through bottom of bowl or colander. Set bowl inside basket and wire together, if necessary, by drilling several ⁵/₃₂" holes around bowl lip.

4. Install lamp kit inside bowl-basket unit according to instructions.

5. Hang flatware from basket with wire.

HeadSTRONG

Her pencil-thin lips drew taut as she eyed me over narrow bifocals. "I im not permeeted to deesturb ze deesplay," she said. "Eef you are serieux, come back when ze windows weel be chan-jay." Unfortunately, I was leaving Paris the next day. After a lengthy discussion, the headstrong clerk sullenly agreed to remove the bag from the display if I vowed to purchase it. With the precision of a surgeon, she began the process of unlocking, unbuckling and unzipping each compartment. "Eet's a Sac Chasse, 'ow you say, un 'unting bagge." She explained every minute detail as she worked. "Oh, a hunting bag, but what a great carry-on it would make!" Her knuckles whitened as they gripped the detachable leather strap. I had to act fast and threw my credit card down to complete the transaction before being asked to get "Ze 'ell out of ze magasin."

This multi-functional headboard boasts all the nighttime amenities required for sweet dreams.

DI*Wise*
Reclaimed doors and shelves contribute to the perfect custom bed accessory.

DIY
$75–100 (SRP $250–300)

COST
$75–100
(SRP $250–300)

TIME
6–8 hours

MATERIALS
2 doors* (should be as wide as bed or wider when stood side by side)

2 kitchen drawers, wine crates or rectangular shelves

2 wall-mounted reading lamps

2 bed pillows with shams

Cording or ribbon for sham loops

Selection of small lipped vases

Paint, stain or furniture wax (optional)

4 door knobs (that include back plates with two screw holes)

4, 2" hinges

$5/8$" and $1^1/2$" wood screws

1" x 3" lumber, 6' long

Wood glue

Clock or clock movement with shaft long enough to penetrate back of shelf unit

Wood filler (optional)

Degreaser (optional)

2 door stops

TOOLS
Drill, $1/2$" drill bit

Jigsaw or table saw

Brush, cloth or roller (if using paint or stain)

Tape measure

Pencil

Goggles

Gloves

Sander, 180-grit sandpaper

*If you purchase doors from a reclaim centre, the knobs and hinges will have been removed but will be on display close by and available for purchase.

REPURPOSE, RECLAIM & REDEFINE LEISURE TIME

STEP BY STEP

1. If painting or staining surfaces, sand shelves. If using cabinet drawers as shelves, remove drawer faces and all hardware. Fill holes with wood filler, if desired, and sand. If shelf units are finished in melamine, sand thoroughly to remove gloss finish and wipe with degreaser to ensure paint adhesion.

2. Position lipped vases in desired locations on top of cabinets and mark. Drill $1/2$" pilot hole and use jigsaw to cut a hole as large as vase diameter. Dry-fit vases and remove.

3. If repurposing an existing clock, take it apart. Mark desired clock location in cabinet; drill an appropriate hole for clock shaft. Dry-fit clock in cabinet and remove.

4. Attach hinges onto cabinet drawers with $5/8$" screws, 3" from top and 3" from bottom on opposing sides (one for right side of bed, one for left). Pre-drill holes with $1/16$" bit, ensuring that you do not drill clear through drawer walls.

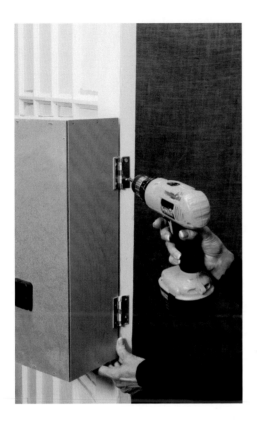

5. Measure bed height and cut doors to desired height. Make sure they will be high enough to allow space for pillows and reading lights. Sand doors; remove any hinges or knobs. Line up recessed mounted sides of doors (where hinges were) face to face.

6. Mark height of bed on doors. Determine height of swinging shelves, which should be about 4–6" higher than mattress. Hold hinged shelf in place and screw hinges to side of door on either side of bed with $1^1/_2$" screws. Cut one piece of 1" x 3" to height of doors. Finish doors, shelves and 1" x 3" as desired.

7. Determine height of pillows and mark for placement of door knobs. (You want them a few inches above pillows.) Attach knobs to doors with $1^1/_2$" screws. Add cord or ribbon loops to pillow shams to align with door knobs.

8. Assemble headboard by screwing cut piece of 1" x 3" against seam between doors. Install reading lamps. Screw door stops to outside lower back side of shelves. Snug up bed to headboard.

NOTE: If shelves are more than three times deeper than headboard, add a two-by-four frame to back of headboard for maximum swing radius.

Horsing Around

After a blur of galleries, museums and the Rialto market, the day ended with a leisurely dinner at Harry's Bar—Hemingway's old haunt and the birthplace of the bellini. As the sun settled over the murky waters of Venice's Grand Canal, we wound our way through the Piazza San Marco amidst audacious pigeons in search of handouts. For nearly 1000 years the Basilica di San Marco has held court in this square. Its fourth-century gilt horses majestically pose over the cathedral's portal entry. Unfortunately, the local feathered populace did not hold the same fascination for Roman antiquity. They frequently met on the sculptures to horse around or voice their concerns over cooing gondoliers serenading passengers with Pavarotti's greatest hits.

Repurpose a set of saw horses into an adjustable table.

DI*Wise*
If you don't already have saw horses, consider making your own with inexpensive bracket kits and two-by-fours available at most hardware outlets.

DIY
$55–75 (SRP $200–275)

○ ○ ●

COST
$55–75
(SRP $200–275)

TIME
6–8 hours

MATERIALS
1 set of saw horses

or

materials to make
2 saw horses:

 2 sets of saw horse
 brackets

 4 two-by-fours,
 8' lengths

 2, 1" x 3" boards,
 8' lengths

 1/2" wood dowel,
 2' length

 11/2" wood dowel,
 4' length

2" wood screws

4, 1/4" x 6" carriage
bolts with 1/4" wing
nuts

Wood glue

3/4" plywood or
MDF (cut to desired
size of table top,
approximately 2' x 4')

Paint or stain (optional)

Furniture wax
(optional)

TOOLS
Drill or drill press,
5/16" drill bit and 9/16"
and 11/2" spade bits

Sander, 220-grit
sandpaper

Paint brush or roller
and tray (optional)

Jigsaw, chop saw
or table saw

Brush or cloth
(optional)

Tape measure

Pencil

Clamps

Level

Mitre box (optional)

Masking tape

REPURPOSE, RECLAIM & REDEFINE LEISURE TIME

STEP BY STEP

SAW HORSES (if making your own)

1. Cut and sand two-by-fours in 16 pieces:

   8 x 27" (legs)
   4 x 26" (crosspieces)
   4 x 12" (braces)

2. Cut and sand $1^1/2$" dowel to make four 12" risers.

3. Cut and sand $^1/2$" dowel to make four 6" pegs.

4. On one crosspiece, mark board centre at $2^1/2$" in from each end. Drill $1^1/2$" holes through board. To make sure crosspieces line up, clamp drilled piece onto another crosspiece to guide drill holes. Repeat with second set of crosspieces.

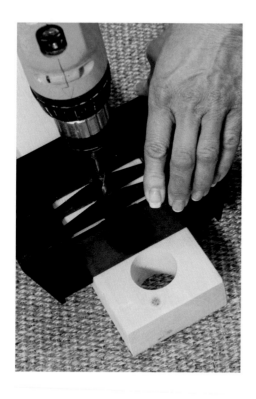

5. Stack two crosspieces and clamp together. Centre brackets on crosspieces to inside of and directly next to bored holes. Using centre hole in bracket as a guide, drill through crosspieces with $^5/_{16}$" bit. Repeat with second set of crosspieces.

6. Clamp two scrap two-by-fours on a drilling surface and snug up tightly on either side of dowel riser piece (lain horizontally) to secure dowel while drilling. Draw centreline along dowel and mark off every 2". Drill $^9/_{16}$" hole through dowel at each mark.

7. Replace hardware that came with bracket system with 6" carriage bolts and $^1/_4$" wing nuts. Construct saw horses following bracket assembly instructions. Drop risers into crosspieces and insert pegs. Fine-tune any adjustments.

8. Push one set of legs as far apart as possible. Measure 8" down from bracket and mark off with a level on both legs. Line up a brace on line and mark off sides as a guide for angle cut required to fit brace between legs. Cut and dry-fit brace. Make any adjustments necessary for a tight support. Using this brace as a guide, cut remaining braces. Dry-fit onto saw horse; do not secure.

TABLE

1. Disassemble saw horses and finish as desired. Reassemble saw horses. Glue and screw braces in place with 2" screws. Finish with two coats of wax (optional).

2. Measure perimeter of table top and mitre-cut 1" x 3" board to appropriate lengths to create a lip. Glue, clamp and tape lip onto table top and dry for four hours.

3. Finish and wax table top as desired. Place on saw horses with corners of table top cupping each dowel riser.

Material Girl

Cole Porter's "I Love Paris in the Spring Time" came to mind as I gazed at Gustav Eiffel's iconic iron tower from our hotel balcony. Across the street a jogger made the rounds on a shale oval surrounded by plane trees and dogwood petals that had blown through the heart of the city. I, on the other hand, was on another mission—one that involved shops, credit cards and a whole lot of bags. But, as the day wore on and my haul increased in weight, I, too, found refuge where gravel pathways led to avenues of chestnut trees that crowned generous benches. It was the perfect place to nurse blisters and fears of overspending. Musicians filled the air with the notes of Chopin while university students read peacefully on statue pedestals. Lovers rolled over one another like tumblers and seniors settled in to catch up on the latest gossip.

Give *joie de vivre* to consoles and tables with a classic slipcover, or add a bit of humour to mundane tablecloths or placemats.

DIWise
Make your own textile paint by combining one part acrylic paint to one part textile medium. Use natural fibres and pre-washed fabric to remove sizing.

DIY
$15–25 (SRP $250–375)

COST
$15–25
(SRP $250 375)

TIME
2–5 hours

MATERIALS
Fabric, bed sheets
or canvas drop
cloths (washed,
dried and ironed)

Plain, light-coloured
placemats (washed,
dried and ironed)

Thread

Fabric or craft paint
and textile medium

Freezer paper
(available at quilting
outlets, online or
from your butcher)

Paper (for template)

Paper towel

TOOLS
Sewing machine

Scissors

Tape measure

Stencil brush

Utility or Exacto
knife

Pencil

Pins

Iron

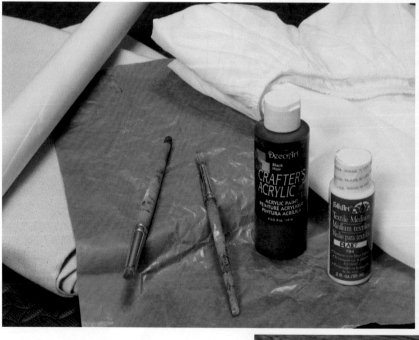

REPURPOSE, RECLAIM & REDEFINE LEISURE TIME

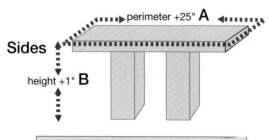

Sides

perimeter +25" **A**

height +1" **B**

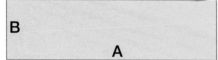

B

A

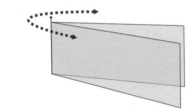

fold fabric in half *widthwise*

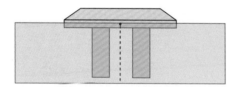

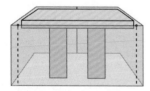

mark *front only* console corners

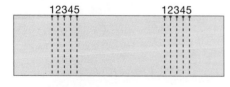

12345   12345

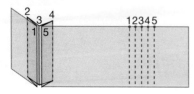

2   4
3
1   5   12345

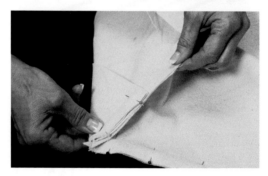

STEP BY STEP

CONSOLE SLIPCOVER

1. You need two pieces of fabric to make this slipcover: one to cover sides of console and one to cover top.

2. For first piece, measure height of console and perimeter of console's top surface. Cut fabric to be 1" wider than measured height and 25" longer than perimeter. Fold fabric in half widthwise to find midpoint. Temporarily attach fabric around edges of console so that midpoint is at centre of console's front side. Mark console's front corners on fabric. To create box pleats, mark and measure in 3" increments, as shown. Pin in place and iron.

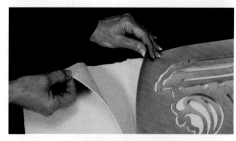

3. Measure table top and cut top fabric large enough to cover table top plus 1" on all sides.

4. Enlarge stencil pattern to desired size and transfer design to paper. Cut out design, and trace in sections onto matte side of freezer paper. You need approximately seven stencils to complete design. Cut with knife or scissors to create stencil. Position stencil on fabric, shiny side down, and iron stencil on high setting.

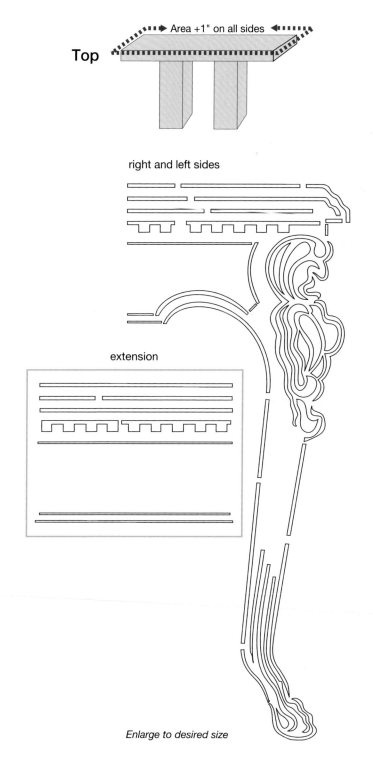

Top

Area +1" on all sides

right and left sides

extension

Enlarge to desired size

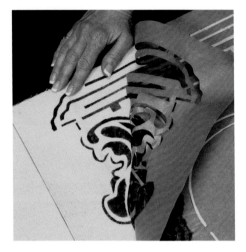

5. If using craft paint and medium, mix according to manufacturer's instructions. Apply textile paint very sparingly to stencil by dabbing lightly with stencil brush. Remove excess paint from brush by blotting on paper towel. Do not overload brush or paint will bleed under stencil. Play with various levels of opacity for inner detailed sections to create depth. Dry one hour. Remove stencil and repeat process with remaining stencils until three sides of console are complete. If back of console will be viewed, finish all four sides. Set paint according to supplier's instructions.

6. With right sides of fabric together, sew back seam of painted fabric and press seam open. Pin top in place and cut corners as shown for smooth finish. Serge or zig-zag seams if desired. Launder slipcover as directed on textile paint instructions.

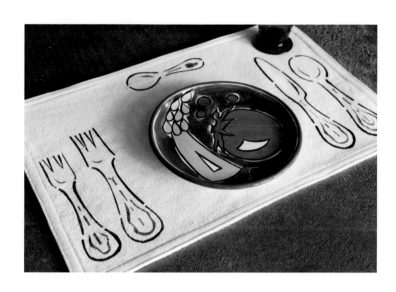

Enlarge to desired size

PLACEMATS

1. Enlarge pattern to desired size and transfer design to paper. Cut out design and trace onto matte side of freezer paper. Cut with knife or scissors to create stencil. Position stencil on fabric, shiny side down, and iron stencil on high setting.

2. If using craft paint and medium, mix according to manufacturer's instructions. Apply textile paint very sparingly to stencil by dabbing lightly with stencil brush. Remove excess paint from brush by blotting on paper towel. Do not overload brush or paint will bleed under stencil. Dry one hour. Remove stencil and repeat process with remaining placemats. Set paint according to supplier's instructions. Launder as directed on textile paint instructions.

Monkey Business

For a dollar you could purchase clusters of fingerling bananas at the entrance of the Sacred Monkey Sanctuary in Ubud, Bali. I bought several, in the hopes of spending the afternoon feeding the band of grey-haired macaques in the midst of the lush tropical surroundings. To my disappointment, the mischievous monkeys were vigilant for passing tourists and devoured the fruit within minutes. Officially named Mandala Wisata Wanara Wana, the forest is also home to three holy temples amid massive trees strangled by figs and hanging vines. I noticed a group of monkeys patiently grooming each other on the steps leading to the Holy Bathing Temple. With practised fingers, they carefully combed for insects and dirt. I turned to share the discovery with H. just in time to see a macaque climb onto his shoulder and gently part his hair to begin the diligent process of preening.

With a little monkeying around, you can transform ordinary spindles into Indonesian-inspired candle pillars.

DI*Wise*
Look for used spindles at architectural clearing centres or flea markets.

DIY
$15–30 (SRP $75–100) for two units

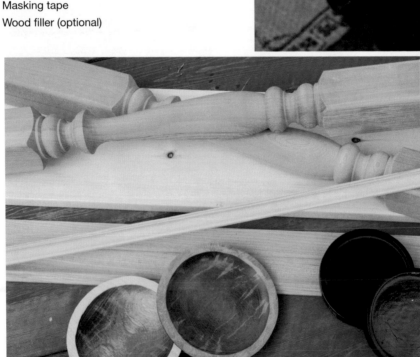

COST
$15–30
(SRP $75–100)
for two units

TIME
3–5 hours

MATERIALS
2 large spindles or
newel posts

1" x 8" board,
4' length

Baseboard trim,
4' length

Detailed trim, 8' length

Paint, stain or oil
(optional)

Small wood or metal
dishes

2¹/₂" common nails

Masking tape

Wood filler (optional)

TOOLS
Handsaw, chop saw
or table saw

Hammer

Wood glue

Mitre box

180-grit sandpaper

Paint brush (optional)

Clamps

Drill, ⁹/₆₄" drill bit

Goggles

Gloves

STEP BY STEP

1. Mitre-cut four pieces of 1" x 8" to make a base around bottom of spindle. Glue pieces to base of spindle and clamp or tape in place.

2. Mitre-cut four pieces of baseboard trim to fit around bottom of 1" x 8" base wrap. Glue and clamp or tape in place.

3. Mitre-cut two sets of detailed trim: four pieces each to fit around top of 1" x 8" base wrap and around bottom of baseboard trim. Glue and clamp or tape in place. Fill gaps or blemishes with wood filler, if desired. Increase pillar stability by gluing a 1" x 8" board under candle base.

4. Drill ⁹/₆₄" hole in centre of dish. Hammer nail into bored hole from underside of dish. Glue onto top of spindle. Weight overnight for even adhesion.

5. Finish candle pillar as desired.

Ruff Day

With our winnings, we left the casinos of Monaco and headed west to Juan-Les-Pins on the Cap d'Antibes. Our destination was the Hôtel Juana, a sumptuous Art Déco property that boasted a Michelin rated restaurant. It was an appropriate address to exhaust our jackpot. An eight-course gastronomic feast awaited us, and we spent an entire evening with an endless bounty of haute cuisine and well-aged wine. As we dined for hours among the literati and glitterati of the French Riviera, a succession of locals filled and emptied the restaurant, often accompanied by pampered pets. Once seated beneath linen lined tables, the pooches were served bottled water in engraved silver bowls. Not surprisingly, the rhinestone-accessorized hounds usually left with swanky doggie bags.

Repurpose a tired ottoman into a multi-tasker chill-out with your feet up while Fido relaxes below.

DI*Wise*
The hinged lid makes it easy to clean up inside, including the routine excavation of buried treasures.

DIY
$35–55 (SRP $95–125)

COST
$35–55
(SRP $95–125)

TIME
4–5 hours

MATERIALS
Ottoman, storage chest or toy chest

2" foam, enough to fit lid of unit

Fabric and batting to cover top and sides of unit

Thread

Upholstery studs and fringe (optional)

2 x 2" hinges

Coroplast, 4 sheets at 2' x 4' or 1 sheet at 4' x 8' (available at hardware store or sign outlet)

Double-sided foam tape

Silicone adhesive

4 small ball fence caps (optional for legs)

Duct tape

Pillow

Uncooked rice, wheat, barley, flax seed or buckwheat hulls (optional)

TOOLS
Sewing machine

Jigsaw

Stapler, with $1/4$" staples

Scissors

Tape measure

Silicone gun

Sander, 150-grit sandpaper

Hammer

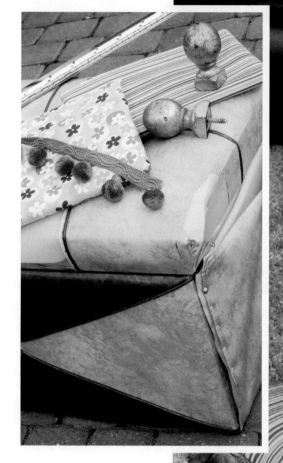

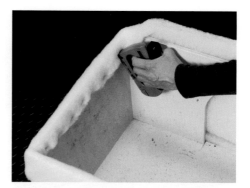

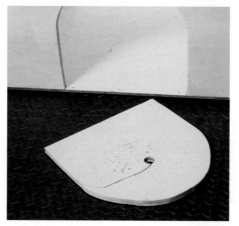

STEP BY STEP

1. Strip existing fabric off ottoman. Remove top (lid) and set aside. Cut inverted U-shaped opening on one side for entrance. Sand if necessary.

2. Wrap sides of unit with batting. Staple in place. Cut batting at opening and staple on inside.

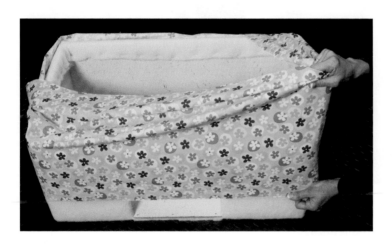 

3. Cut fabric to size for sides by adding
   1" to length measurement and 4" to
   width. Sew along short edges, wrong
   sides together. Dry-fit around unit
   base to ensure a tight fit. If it is loose,
   adjust accordingly. Pull fabric over
   unit, leaving 2" of excess fabric at
   top and bottom. Staple excess fabric
   taut on inside of unit. Cut fabric at
   opening and staple on inside.

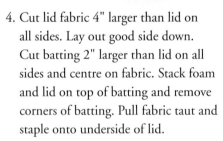

4. Cut lid fabric 4" larger than lid on all sides. Lay out good side down. Cut batting 2" larger than lid on all sides and centre on fabric. Stack foam and lid on top of batting and remove corners of batting. Pull fabric taut and staple onto underside of lid.

5. Create a lid liner by cutting a piece of Coroplast slightly smaller than lid. Cut fabric 2" larger than Coroplast and affix with duct tape. Adhere liner to lid with double-sided tape and silicone. Attach hinges to lid and base, if desired.

6. Cut four Coroplast pieces to fit snugly inside unit on sides. Cut another piece to fit on bottom of unit. Adhere Coroplast pieces with double-sided tape and silicone. Sew removable slipcover for pillow and place on floor of ottoman.

7. Embellish unit with upholstery studs or fringe, if desired.

If you have any scraps of fabric and trim left over, sew a small pillow and stuff it with uncooked rice, wheat, barley, flax seed or buckwheat hulls. Microwave or freeze the cushion to provide hot or cold therapy for sore or aged muscles and joints.

Some Like It Haute

On my first trip to Hungary, my father escorted me to his birthplace in the picturesque village of Csongrád, a few hours south of Budapest. Time had stood still in Csongrád: the houses and streets had remained practically untouched for 50 years. Dad's childhood home was still standing. In fact, my grandfather's name was clearly legible in raised letters above the front door despite 75 years of exposure to the elements. The present occupants graciously invited us in for seltzer and *málnaszörp* (raspberry syrup) made from raspberries harvested from the original garden. The main bedroom had not changed since the day my dad was born in it in the summer of 1927. The floor-to-ceiling stove stood resplendently in the corner of the white-washed room. Its sage green tile was still gleaming. The image of that ornately tiled wood-burning stove stayed with me and eventually materialized in my kitchen—in the form of a cooler cover.

Update your utilitarian water dispenser with a new, colourful wrap.

DI*Wise*
Use a large platter to crown your cooler wrap. It can serve as a base for a ready supply of glasses.

DIY
$50–75 (SRP $200–275)

COST
$50–75
(SRP $200–275)

TIME
8–14 hours

MATERIALS
Sonotube, 3" wider
than cooler diameter,
approximately 5' long

Mosaic tiles
(1" or 2" square)

Tile adhesive

Grout

Grout sealant

Piano hinge
(approximately 4' long)
and piano hinge
screws

1" x 1" wood slats,
8 x 5' lengths

Plastic U-shaped
edging (available
in cabinetry
department of
hardware stores)

Velcro, $1/2$" x 5'
(both hook and
loop parts)

TOOLS
Jigsaw or
utility knife

Tile cutter

Glue gun and glue
sticks

Tile trowel

Brush

Scissors

Blow dryer or heat
gun

Drill, $1/16$" drill bit

Clamps

STEP BY STEP

1. Use jigsaw or utility knife to cut Sonotube to 4" longer than height of cooler. Cut tube in half lengthwise so you are left with two identical units.

2. Cut an opening in one half of Sonotube for access to water levers. Cut an opening in other half for cooling and ventilation. Using utility knife to cut plastic edging to size, finish openings and all edges on Sonotube. Use heat gun or blow dryer set on high to soften and round edging pieces as necessary to conform to tube curvature. Use hot glue to fix plastic edging to Sonotubes.

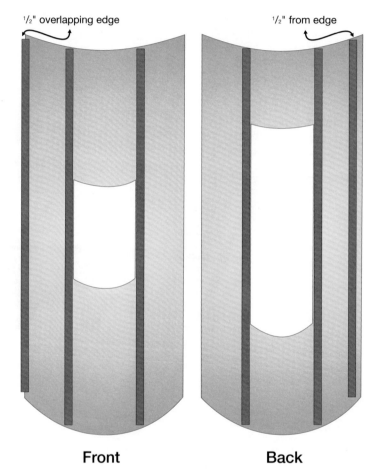

½" overlapping edge   ½" from edge

Front   **Back**

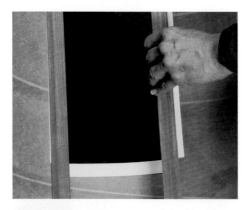

3. Cut eight wood slats to 1" shorter than Sonotube.

4. Clamp hinge in place and mark off holes with drill from inside Sonotube. Place wood slat over hinge on inside and clamp. Screw hinge in place from outside Sonotube using pilot holes as guide. Repeat process on other tube half. Use hot glue to fix wood slats to inside of tubes, as shown in illustration.

5. Affix Velcro to exposed wood lip on one side and to edge of Sonotube on opposite side. Close Sonotube around cooler.

6. Tile exterior of Sonotube with mosaic tiles, starting pattern from centre of each tube half. Bevel tile edges along hinged and opens length of tube to prevent chipping. Dry for 24 hours and then apply grout. Cure for 24 hours and then seal with two coats of grout sealant.

7. Top cooler cover with large platter to hold water glasses.

Suitable Impression

A taxì libero was parked just across the cobbled
street, but after three hours of dining, H. and I
needed the walk. Loosening our belts we fell into
step with the pedestrian flow as the evening air
unfolded around us, spiced with the aroma of
roasting chestnuts. The streets of Florence were
perpetually busy, regardless of the time of day or
night. Extravagant boutiques presented legendary
designer lines and unparalleled window shopping.
Linked arm-in-arm, young couples looked like
runway models on the Piazza San Marco as they
paraded by in Gucci and Fiorucci. Restaurants
spilled onto sidewalks, where Armani and Versace
dined harmoniously under striped canopies.
Espresso-fuelled drivers screamed by amid the
hoards of Vespa's zigzagging traffic in a chorus of
honking horns and animated gestures. Our hotel
was finally in sight. Unfortunately, it was across the
street. Bravely, we grabbed each other's hand and
ran for dear life.

Create a toasty blanket or cushion slipcovers from outdated suits or sports jackets.

DI*Wise*
Used designer labels still demand a hefty price tag, but thrift shops are a great place to find suits and sports jackets. Alternately, menswear retailers might have suit samples that are the perfect size for quilting.

DIY
$45–75 (SRP $200–275)

COST
$45–75
(SRP $200–275)

TIME
8–10 hours

MATERIALS
Outdated suits or
sports jackets, or
sample suit pieces

Thread

Embroidery floss
(optional)

Fabric for slipcover
lining and quilt
backing

Quilt batting

Elastic mattress stays

TOOLS
Sewing machine

Scissors

Darning needle

Tape measure

Iron

Pins

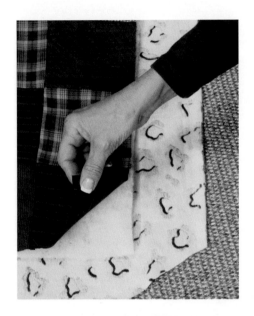

STEP BY STEP

QUILT

1. Cut suit pieces into uniform, 5" x 5" squares.

2. Machine stitch squares together until you have made a cover in desired size. Cut batting to same size as quilted piece. Cut quilt backing fabric 2½" larger on all sides than quilted piece.

3. Centre quilt and batting on backing fabric. Cut off corners on backing as shown. Fold backing over quilt front and top-stitch in place with ½" roll hem.

4. Embellish quilt seams with embroidery floss, if desired.

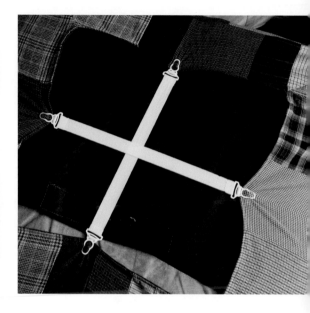

STEP BY STEP

SOFA CUSHION SLIPCOVERS

1. Cut suit pieces into $3^{1}/_{2}"$ x $3^{1}/_{2}"$, $3^{1}/_{2}"$ x $6^{1}/_{2}"$, and $6^{1}/_{2}"$ x $6^{1}/_{2}"$ pieces.

2. Measure top and sides of sofa cushions. Stitch together suit pieces to create a slipcover 6" larger on all sides. Centre cushion on slipcover and pin corners for a snug fit. Cut off excess fabric, remove pins, remove slipcover from cushion and cut a duplicate from lining fabric. Stitch corners on slipcover and lining. Put slipcover on cushion and pin mitred corners on back of cushion as shown. Remove and stitch. Repeat with lining.

3. With wrong sides together, stitch lining and slipcover together, leaving 12" opening at one end. Turn inside out through opening and top-stitch opening closed.

4. Place cushion in slipcover and secure with mattress stays.

Swiss Movements

The room at the Savoy in Zurich was small but generously appointed. It had a roomy balcony framed by a weave of ironwork. The terrace overlooked Bahnhofstrasse, a street lined with posh stores and even posher banks. We opted to dine alfresco and spend the evening people watching from our sixth-floor vantage point. As the evening settled into night, hourly choruses of the city's clock towers chimed in unison, reaffirming that there is indeed one clock face for every three residents in Switzerland. Zurich was not a bad place to have forgotten your watch, particularly because it is home to the largest clock face in Europe: it is on the St. Peterskirche church, measures $28^{1}/_{2}'$ in diameter and has a delicate, $12'$ long minute hand.

Create your own version of a showy, XXXL clock with a ceiling medallion.

DI_Wise_
Scour garage sales or architectural clearing houses to find a relic medallion to resurrect.

DIY
$25–30 (SRP $95–125)

COST
$35–55
(SRP $150–200)

TIME
2–3 hours

MATERIALS
Ceiling medallion with centre insert

Paint or stain (optional)

Clock movement with hands and extended shaft

Wire

1½" screw eyes

Silicone adhesive

TOOLS
Drill, ³⁄₈" spade bit

Paint brush and rags (if painting or staining)

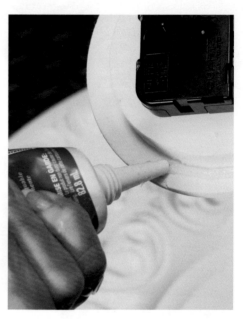

STEP BY STEP

1. Drill hole in centre of insert with spade bit.

2. Install clock movement on insert according to package instructions. Join insert and medallion with silicone adhesive.

3. Paint or stain desired effect on medallion and insert. To achieve a faux finish on this clock, spray medallion and insert with black paint. Dry several hours. Mix a patina of two parts water to one part metallic craft paint. Paint on surface and wipe off excess with a dry cloth.

4. Attach hanging wire on back of unit with screw eyes.

Do It Yourself

THE MUST HAVES

Hammer and assorted nails

Electric drill and assorted drill bits

Screwdrivers and assorted screws

Pliers

Scissors, utility knife and blades

Wire cutters

Straight edge, square and level

Tape measure

Pencil or chalk

Handsaw and hacksaw

Stapler and staples

Sanding block and sandpapers

Toolbox

Gloves, mask, safety goggles and ear protection

HANDY & HELPFUL

Jigsaw and circular saw

Specialized drill bits (e.g., Forstner) and paddle attachment

Caulking gun

Glue gun and glue sticks

Clamps

Wood and metal files

Tile cutter, nippers, notched trowel and spatulas

Large utility pails

Paint brushes, rollers, trays and rags

DIYER'S WISH LIST

Band saw

Chop saw or cut-off saw

Portable table saw

Drill press

Belt sander

Dremel tool

7" wet saw

Shop vacuum

Angle grinder

I want to remind you that if you're lacking a skill or a tool, staff at a hardware store can be quite accommodating. Just ask them to cut lumber or pipe for you. If you are going to use a specialty tool once, borrow it from a friend or neighbour, or rent it for an afternoon instead of forking out the dough to buy it. And if you're not into foraging in the woods for twigs, branches or other organic supplies, don't forget about your local garden centre or craft outlet.

THE WORKSHOP

A workshop can be as elaborate as a stand-alone studio or as simple as a corner in a spare bedroom. Good light, ventilation and a bit of space to spread out and move about are essential. If you have young children or inquisitive pets, a room with a locking door is a must.

Working on a raised surface will save serious wear and tear on your back. Customize the height of your work surface by raising it up on blocks, and expand accessibility by adding locking casters. You can fabricate a basic workbench from saw horses and a sheet of plywood so it can be taken down for storage when not needed. Using a swing-arm desk lamp can enhance overhead lighting. If you are working outside, picnic tables or potting benches can serve double duty as sturdy worktops.

My workshop is an organized, defined space where I spend a lot of time. I purchased and installed rubber floor tiles from the hardware store, and they're warm and comfortable to stand on. When I'm not standing, I have a tall stool to perch on, and I keep a folding stepladder nearby to retrieve items stored high up in the old kitchen cabinets I've mounted on the walls. I keep a stack of drop sheets to protect surfaces in case I need to spread a project out on the floor. I use a large bin for garbage, but, in order to save my back, I never overfill it. Another bin neatly contains scraps of lumber. I'm big on safety (see Safety Do's and Don'ts, page 115) and keep all of my safety equipment close at hand. I also have music playing, which adds to an enjoyable atmosphere.

SAFETY DO'S AND DON'TS

Take the time to review the following safety tips to avoid trips to the emergency department. It is essential that you keep safety in mind while working on a project. As a bonus, you'll look like a pro with all the gear.

1. **Wear safety goggles, work gloves and a dust mask** when working with power tools, sanders, saws or paint. Always wear hearing protection when operating loud or repetitive equipment.

2. **Equip your workshop with a fire extinguisher** and periodically check the charge. Keep a well-stocked first aid kit on hand. A basic first aid poster is great in an emergency, as is a shop phone.

3. **If possible, work outdoors** when painting, sanding or cutting materials. If it is too cold, work indoors in a well-ventilated space.

4. **Always cut away from yourself** when using cutting tools.

5. **Unplug power tools** when changing blades or bits, or when cleaning. Don't use electrical tools outside when it's raining. Check that all electrical cords are in good shape. It may be well worth the effort to have damaged cords replaced on good power tools, but don't put this task off.

6. **Ladders are a main cause of DIY accidents.** Position ladders on flat, firm surfaces, and keep your weight centred. Never stand on the top two rungs.

7. **Dispose of rubbish carefully.** Before disposing of rags soaked with paint thinner or other flammable liquids, lay them out flat to dry, just as you would a favourite sweater. Carelessness may lead to fire because of spontaneous combustion.

8. **Don't wear loose clothing or open-toed shoes.** Fabric can catch on machinery, and a dropped tool or piece of lumber can really hurt your feet.

DI*Wise*
Safety doesn't happen by accident.

9. **Read all instructions and warning labels** on tools and materials before using for the first time. Keep operating manuals organized in an easy-to-access place.

10. **Keep the workshop floor clear and clean** to avoid tripping or slipping. Coil and hang electrical cords, sweep up messes promptly, and store brooms upright or mounted on the wall.

DOING IT RIGHT

Here are a few tips, tidbits and tactics intended to save time and make any job more pleasurable. It's always easier to learn from the trials and tribulations of others.

1. **Find a partner to split material costs.** Some projects require just a few metres of lumber or small amounts of cement, but you may only be able to purchase these supplies in standard lengths or quantities.

2. **Get your head around a project before you start.** Read through the instructions from start to finish. This step will save time, eliminate nasty surprises and reduce frustration levels.

3. **The French call it *mise en place*—everything in place.** In relation to cooking it refers to gathering, measuring and cutting all of the ingredients required for a recipe before you begin cooking. Applied to DIY, it means setting out all the tools and materials needed before starting a project.

4. **Lay out all your patterns before cutting** to be sure to make the most of your materials with as little waste as possible.

5. **Only a fool rushes in.** Pay attention to drying and curing schedules and follow recommended time frames. Failure to do so could result in peeling, bubbling or shrinkage.

6. **Remember to recycle, repurpose and reuse.** Baskets and battens, sticks and stones, and vents and vessels can all be transformed into something marvellous.

7. **Pace yourself.** If the loud gurgle echoing from your tummy reminds you that dinner was two hours ago, stop and pack up for the day. Remember, you are trying to have fun. Save your enthusiasm for the next session and go have a bite to eat.

8. **These projects do not have to outlive your great grandchildren,** be impervious to the elements or be Superman strong. Their role is to enhance your lifestyle through personal creativity. Remember, you can always whip up a replacement.

SOURCES
Track down materials, textiles, embellishments and antiques at the following sources:

Antique shops and flea markets

Architectural clearing houses

Auctions and bazaars

Big-box chains and hardware outlets

Consignment shops and pawnshops

Craft and hobby retailers

Dollar stores

Estate and garage sales

Fabric shops

Habitat for Humanity ReStores

Upholstery suppliers

DI*Wise*
Critical path thinking saves time, tempers and thumbs.

TIMBERRRRR

WORKING WITH WOOD

You don't have to be a master carpenter to coax a creation from wood. This organic and forgiving medium lends itself to a variety of functions, which can be achieved with the simplest of tools.

1. **Consider safety and your well-being at all times.** Protect your hearing when working with loud or repetitive machinery. Don safety goggles when cutting, drilling or sanding wood. Look for impact-resistant lenses, preferably those with side screens for the ultimate protection. Use a mask or respirator when sanding or cutting wood, particularly when working with pressure-treated wood. Avoid injury when working with power tools by wearing long, tailored sleeves, pants and proper footwear.

2. **Take time at the lumber store** to choose straight, knot-free pieces of wood. Whenever possible, store lumber horizontally to prevent warping. Sand off markers and stamps before you begin cutting.

3. **To drive screws easily into wood and prevent splitting, pre-drill pilot holes** half the diameter of the screw size in hard woods, and one-quarter the diameter in soft woods.

4. **When drilling holes in wood, back the piece with scrap wood to minimize splintering when the bit breaks through.** Clear chips from the hole as you drill to keep the bit working at maximum capacity and allow clear visibility.

5. **Measure twice, cut once—really.** Cut your wood with the "best face" down when using a circular or chop saw, and cut with the "best face" up when using a table saw. Apply masking tape over cutting lines to prevent splintering.

6. **To cut a large opening in a sheet of wood, begin by tracing your pattern onto the wood.** Drill a pilot hole in the centre of your pattern with a drill bit large enough to accommodate a jigsaw blade. Put the blade in the pilot hole and follow the traced pattern.

7. **Always sand with the grain of wood using even strokes and pressure.** Remove dust with a tack cloth or damp rag. Do not be tempted to purchase the least expensive sandpaper available. You will end up using more sheets for the task and a great deal of time changing the paper on your sander. Buy aluminum oxide paper; in the long run it will save money, time and your nerves.

8. **For smooth, even surfaces, fill gaps and open-grained woods with exterior wood filler.** Use a small spatula to apply wood filler and work it into crevices. Once the wood filler loses its sheen and begins to harden, remove any excess with a damp cloth. Sand surfaces smooth. If necessary, repeat the process until the desired effect is achieved.

9. **Be sure to use exterior-grade wood glues for wood-based projects that will be used outdoors.** Also choose galvanized hardware, nails and screws that won't rust.

10. **Wood can be finished with a variety of products: stain, paint, polyurethane varnish or oil.** Keep wood scraps to use as testers for finishes. If you're custom blending your paint or stain, be sure to write down your recipes.

THE TILE FILE

WORKING WITH TILE

Installing ceramic tile is easy with fast-setting thinset or mastic adhesives, grout and sealants. Whatever style or size of tile you choose to install, the principles are the same. Tools and materials include work gloves, rubber gloves, adhesive, grout sealer, tiles, a grooved trowel, a grout float, tile nippers, a tile cutter, a rubber squeegee, a sponge and a level. Inspiration for designs can come from a wide range of sources, from a favourite dinner plate to a grand museum mosaic.

1. **Safety is always the first consideration.** Wear goggles and well-fitted work gloves when cutting tile. Tile edges are sharp, and small shards can cause serious damage to your eyes.

2. **Be sure that the surface to be tiled is free of loose dirt, dust, peeling paint and grease.** Scuff with sandpaper. Apply two coats of Red Gard waterproofing membrane to the base surface if project will be exposed to water.

3. **Conduct a dry run with your tiles by laying out your design and cutting all pieces before adhering.** You can do this directly on the piece to be tiled or you can use an identically sized scrap piece. The latter choice allows you to work smoothly without fear of disturbing the design. Mark two centre lines vertically and horizontally on your surface to act as a guide for your design.

4. **A manual tile cutter can easily handle most cutting jobs,** but if you are cutting a lot of tiles and have access to a wet saw, it can save time.

5. **Mix thinset or mastic adhesive according to manufacturer's instructions.** Spread as much adhesive as you'll be able to cover with tiles in a half hour. As you progress, spread more adhesive as needed. Apply with a notched trowel, holding the trowel at a 45-degree angle. The notches on the trowel help to ensure an even distribution of adhesive. Starting on the middle cross-line reference, transfer the tiles onto the adhesive, gently pressing down. Leave a ¼" gap between tiles or use plastic tile spacers for even distances. Periodically check your work to make sure that tiles are level.

6. **Clean up any excess thinset or mastic from work area with warm water.** Allow adhesives to dry 24 hours before grouting.

7. **Mix grout according to the manufacturer's instructions.** Spread a liberal amount of grout onto the tile and work it into the joints with a grout float. Hold the float at a 45-degree angle and spread the grout in several directions to ensure it settles into all the gaps.

8. **When grout sets up and forms a haze on the tile,** use a damp sponge to wipe away the excess from the tile surface.

9. **Allow the grout to cure based on the manufacturer's recommendations**; then apply two or three coats of grout sealant.

STICKY SITUATIONS

WORKING WITH ADHESIVES

Glue is a DIYer's best friend and the most common fastener. Using the proper adhesive for a project will ensure a successful result. Read the instructions on the label for the appropriate applications and use.

1. **Glues often have specific storage temperature ranges** that help them maintain their effectiveness. This means if your workshop reaches freezing temperatures, you should store glue elsewhere.

2. **Wait for excess wood glue to gel before removing from around joins.** Wiping before gelling will spread adhesive into wood and require extra sanding. Use small paint brushes or wood scraps to spread glue. Always wipe the spouts of containers and replace lids securely after use.

3. **Multi-purpose spray adhesives work best when applied in light, thorough coatings.** Place the project on a drop sheet for easy clean-up of any overspray. Clean nozzles after use by tipping the can upside down and spraying until adhesive does not emit, then wiping the nozzle with a cloth. Work in a well-ventilated area.

4. **Keep heated glue guns upright to prevent damaging the thermostat.** Use hot glue with extreme caution—keep a bowl of cold water handy in case of a burn. Remove glue hairs with a hair dryer set on its hottest temperature.

5. **When using caulk, lay a thin bead of material using steady motion and applying constant pressure.** Smooth the bead and remove excess caulk with the tip of a spoon or the corner of a credit card. Tidy up any lap marks with a moist finger.

PAINTS AND TINTS

WORKING WITH COLOURANT

The finishing touches of any project are the most rewarding. Paints, stains, sealants and waxes can add depth, the impression of years of wear or a gentle patina. Always use exterior finishes for any projects intended for outdoors.

1. **Wear gloves, a respirator and goggles** when painting, staining or sealing. Use spray paints in a well-ventilated room or outdoors on a still day.

2. **Opt for paints that are water-based** or display a low VOC (volatile organic compound) content. VOCs are solvents that evaporate and contribute to the depletion of the ozone.

3. **Take empty paint cans to a recycling depot** that handles both the container and its contents. Never pour paint thinner or paint down the drain.

4. **Tightly fasten lids on paint cans and store upside down.** This treatment will form a seal around the lid to keep paint fresh and ease the process of mixing when you set the can upright for use. For an airtight closure, place a layer of plastic wrap over the opening before tapping the lid into place. Do not allow paint, stain, wax or varnish to freeze.

5. **Avoid clogged spray paint nozzles** by turning the can upside down and spraying until the stream turns clear, then wiping the nozzle with a cloth.

6. **If you plan to paint a project over several days, wrap your brush, roller or paint tray in plastic to keep surfaces moist.** For smaller projects, cover paint trays with plastic wrap before adding paint and, when finished, simply discard the wrap for a quick clean-up.

7. **When you are painting, work logically.** Paint and stain with the grain. Always paint, stain or seal the back or bottom of a project first to prevent scratching or marring on the front face. Elevate your work from the working surface to prevent sticking or drips from accumulating on edges. Styrofoam blocks are handy for supporting screws and hardware while you paint. Clamps or vices wrapped in plastic will hold unstable items steady while you work.

8. **Allow surfaces to dry thoroughly between coats.** If necessary, lightly sand and wipe between coats.

9. **Create your own custom colours** by adding universal professional tints to paints. These colourants are available wherever paints are sold and come in handy 4-oz. tubes. You can also add tints to wax to create darker shades for an aged finish.

10. **Seal a project with wax** to produce a subtle old-world sheen.

Index

A

adhesive 120

B

bags 14

basket, flower 54

batting 88, 102

beads 10

bed springs 3

beeswax 16, 48

birds 6, 12

blanket 101

board, cutting 16, 47

bottle 3, 20

bottles 19

bowl, mixing 54

breadboard 48

bubble wrap 14

C

cabinet 42

caps, fence 36, 88

cardboard 14

chair 28, 41

chairs 27

chandelier 53

charm 24

chest 42

chest, toy 88

chopstick 6

clock 18, 60, 107, 108

cloths, drop 74

coasters 23

colander 54

colouring, food 16

cooler 95

corks 3, 16, 20

Coroplast 88

crate, wine 3, 36, 60

curtains 22

D

daybed 35

dishes 82

dispenser, water 95

doors, reclaimed 59, 60

dowel 36, 66

drawers 60

driftwood 28

D-rings 14

E

extinguisher, fire 115

F

fabric 22, 88, 102

fabric, sheer 36

fabric, upholstery 36

feeder 6,12

foam 88

forks 54

fridge 8

G

glass 20

glass, wine 16

gloves 118, 121

goggles 115, 121

grout 96, 119

H

hanger, coat 6, 12

headboard 59

hinge, piano 42, 96

horses, saw 66

J

jackets, sports 101, 102

jeans 14

K

knobs, door 60

L

ladder 41, 115

ladle 12, 53, 54

lamps 60

lamp kit 7, 54

light 7

lumber 117

M

magnet 8

marbles 10

measurements xviii

medallion, ceiling 108

mesh, stucco 10

mirror 9

O

ottoman 87, 88

P

painting 115

paints 120

paper, freezer 74

patio 27

pennies 11

pillars, candle 81

pillow 36, 60, 88

placemats 73, 74

platter 95

plywood 12, 66

posts, newel 82

pull, drawer 48

putty 28

Q

quilt, 100

R

recycle 116

respirator 121

rod, threaded 28

rub, metallic wax 54

S

safety 115

sanding 115

sealant 119, 120

sheeting, magnetic 8

sheets, bed 74

sieve 48, 53

skewers, bamboo 2, 16

skill level xviii

slipcover 73, 101, 102

solder 11

Sonotube 96

sources 116

spindles 36, 81, 82

spoons 7, 53, 54

SRP xviii

stains 120

stays, elastic mattress 102

stick, stir 18

Styrofoam 2

suits 102

supplies 113

T

table 42, 65

tablecloths 73

tassels 10

tea lights 11

tiara 9

tile 19, 96, 118, 119

tin 7, 18

tin, olive oil 2

tin, tuna 6

tools 113, 115

tray 16

tubes, cigar 22, 23

tubes, test 22, 23

tubes, vanilla bean 22, 23

V

vase 10, 19, 24, 60

Velcro 36, 96

vinyl, self-adhesive 8, 9, 24

W

weather stripping 23

whisk 18

window 22

wood 117

workshop 114, 115

Z

zipper 24

Acknowledgements

Thank you to the following people who were
fundamental in putting this book together:

Akemi Matsubuchi, for your brilliant photography,
patience and friendship.

Karen McVean, Jadeene Wheaton and Gordon Mueller,
for the use of your private sanctuaries.

Julie Wheaton, for your enthusiastic modelling.

My mother, Lilli Bodo, for unwavering support and
pitching in whenever needed.

Bill and Valerie Hole and Bruce Timothy Keith of Hole's
Publishing, for their expertise and guidance.

Lee Craig, for your discerning editing.

Carol Dragich, for your brilliant layouts and cover design.

And finally, Joseph Bodo, who taught me to never quit.